Editor
Heather Douglas

Illustrator
Kelly McMahon

Cover Artist
Barb Lorseyedi

Editor in Chief
Ina Massler Levin, M.A

Creative Director
Karen J. Goldfluss, M.S. Ed.

Art Coordinator
Renée Mc Elwee

Imaging
Craig Gunnell

Publisher
Mary D. Smith, M.S. Ed.

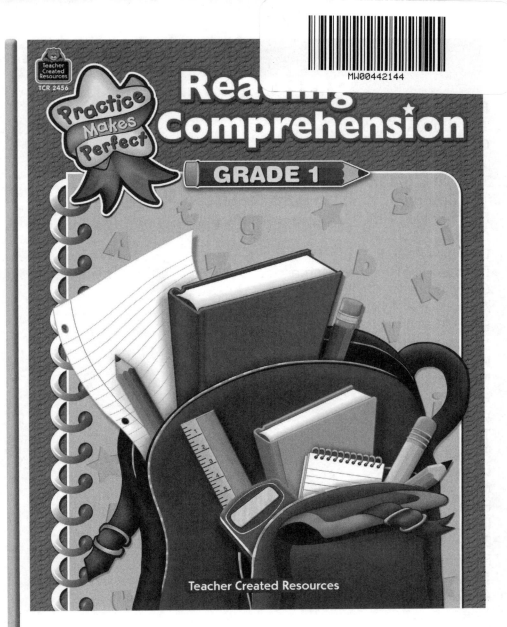

TCR 2456

Practice Makes Perfect

Reading Comprehension

GRADE 1

Teacher Created Resources

Author
Becky Wood

Teacher Created Resources
12621 Western Avenue
Garden Grove, CA 92841
www.teachercreated.com

ISBN: 978-1-4206-2456-8

©2011 Teacher Created Resources
Reprinted, 2016
Made in U.S.A.

Teacher Created Resources

Table of Contents

Introduction

The old adage "practice makes perfect" can really hold true for your child and his or her education. The more practice and exposure your child has with concepts being taught in school, the more success he or she is likely to find. For many parents, knowing how to help their children may be frustrating because the resources may not be readily available.

As a parent it is also difficult to know where to focus your efforts so that the extra practice your child receives at home supports what he or she is learning in school.

This book has been written to help parents and teachers reinforce basic skills with children. *Practice Makes Perfect: Reading Comprehension Grade 1* gives practice in reading and answering questions to help fully comprehend what is read. The exercises in this book can be done sequentially or can be taken out of order, as needed.

After reading the story the questions can be answered either by filling in the bubbles on the same page with a pencil or crayon or using the answer sheet found on page 46.

The following standards and objectives are similar to the ones required by your state and school district. These standards and objectives are appropriate for the first grade.

- Understands level-appropriate sight words and vocabulary

- Uses reading skills and strategies to understand a variety of familiar literary passages and texts

- Uses reading skills and strategies to understand a variety of informational texts

How to Make the Most of This Book

Here are some useful ideas for making the most of this book:

- Set aside a specific place in your home to work on this book. Keep it neat and tidy with materials ready on hand.

- Set up a certain time of day to work on these practice pages to establish consistency, or look for times in your day or week that are less hectic and conducive to practicing skills.

- Keep all practice sessions with your child positive and constructive. If the mood becomes frustrated or tense, set the book aside for another time. This is especially important for emerging readers.

- If the story is too hard, consider reading the story and questions with your child. Allow the child to do more and more of the reading as his or her skill increases.

- Review the work your child has done.

- Allow the child to use whatever writing instruments he or she prefers: pencils, colored pencils, or crayons.

- Pay attention to the areas in which your child has the most difficulty. Provide extra guidance and exercises in those areas.

Name_____

The Birthday Party

Billy had a birthday party. He opened presents. He played games. He ate cake and ice cream. It was a great day.

1. Who had a birthday?
Ⓐ Billy
Ⓑ Lisa
Ⓒ Sam

2. What did he do first?
Ⓐ ate cake and ice cream
Ⓑ opened presents
Ⓒ played games

3. Did Billy have a fun day?
Ⓐ yes
Ⓑ no

Camping

Sam likes to go camping in the woods.
When it gets dark, it is time to go to bed.
He rolls out his sleeping bag and puts it in
the tent. He thinks it is fun to sleep outside
in a tent at night.

1. Where does Sam like to go
camping?

  Ⓐ   in the woods

  Ⓑ   at the beach

  Ⓒ   in the backyard

2. What does he put in his tent?

  Ⓐ   food

  Ⓑ   a sleeping bag

  Ⓒ   a toy

3. Where does he sleep?

  Ⓐ   in a house

  Ⓑ   in a tent

  Ⓒ   in a tree

Name_____

The New Bike

Mike got a new bike for his birthday. It is red and black and very fast. When Mike rides down the street, he rings the bell on his bike so everyone will know he is coming. He loves his bike.

1. What did Mike get for his birthday?

Ⓐ a boat

Ⓑ a bike

Ⓒ a plane

2. What color is his bike?

Ⓐ orange and blue

Ⓑ yellow and green

Ⓒ red and black

3. What does he ring to tell people he is coming?

Ⓐ a phone

Ⓑ a bell

Ⓒ an alarm clock

The Cat in the Tree

Sally saw a cat up in the tree. She ran to get her mother to help. Her mom got a ladder and lifted the cat out of the tree. Sally was glad she could help the cat.

1. What did Sally see?
   - (A) a cat
   - (B) a bird
   - (C) a squirrel

2. Who did she get to help?
   - (A) her mother
   - (B) her friend
   - (C) her dad

3. What did her mom use to reach the cat?
   - (A) a box
   - (B) a ladder
   - (C) a chair

Name_____

The Balloon

Dan went to a party. He got a big green balloon. He gave the balloon to his little sister. She was very happy.

1. What did Dan get at the party?
   - (A) a piece of cake
   - (B) a big green balloon
   - (C) a bouncy ball

2. Who did he give it to?
   - (A) his friend
   - (B) his brother
   - (C) his sister

3. How did his sister feel?
   - (A) happy
   - (B) sad
   - (C) angry

Name_____

Puppies for Sale

**Josh had a dog that had five puppies.
His mom and dad said he could not keep
all of the puppies. He put them in a
basket. Then he wrote, "Puppies for Sale."**

1. Who had a dog?
   - Ⓐ Josh
   - Ⓑ John
   - Ⓒ Mike

2. Where did he put the puppies?
   - Ⓐ in a basket
   - Ⓑ in a box
   - Ⓒ in a closet

3. What did he write?
   - Ⓐ I like puppies.
   - Ⓑ Puppies for Sale
   - Ⓒ Come look at my puppies.

Name_____

Clouds

Zachary likes to look at white fluffy clouds in the blue sky. Sometimes he likes to find pictures in the clouds. Look! That cloud looks like a turtle.

1. Who likes to look at white fluffy clouds?

  (A) Jeremy

  (B) Zachary

  (C) Logan

2. What does he like to find in them?

  (A) numbers

  (B) pictures

  (C) people

3. What does one of the clouds look like?

  (A) a train

  (B) a boat

  (C) a turtle

Lost and Found

Sarah lost her jacket at school yesterday. Her mom said she had to look for it. She looked in her classroom and out in the hall. She found it on the playground by the slide. She was glad she found her jacket.

1. Who lost her jacket at school yesterday?

(A) Jane

(B) Jill

(C) Sarah

2. Where did she look?

(A) in the classroom and out in the hall

(B) in the gym

(C) in the lunchroom

3. Where did she find it?

(A) in the gym

(B) in the lunchroom

(C) on the playground by the slide

Name_____

David's First Baseball Game

**Monday is David's first baseball game.
He is very excited. His coach has told his
team all the rules. His team worked hard.
Now it is time to play.**

---

1. When is David's first game?

  Ⓐ Saturday

  Ⓑ Sunday

  Ⓒ Monday

2. Who told his team all the rules?

  Ⓐ his dad

  Ⓑ his coach

  Ⓒ his friend

3. What has the team done?

  Ⓐ worked hard

  Ⓑ goofed off

  Ⓒ not listened

Camping in the Backyard

Rachel likes to set up her tent in the backyard. It is a fun place to sleep at night. She can look out the tent window and see the moon and stars. Then she can get in her sleeping bag and go to sleep.

1. Where does Rachel like to set up tent?
   - (A) at the beach
   - (B) in her backyard
   - (C) at her school

2. What can she look out the tent window to see?
   - (A) the sun
   - (B) the trees
   - (C) the moon and the stars

3. What does she get into to go to sleep?
   - (A) her sleeping bag
   - (B) her bed
   - (C) a blanket

A Trip to the Zoo

Jason likes to go to the zoo. He sees the monkeys, the birds, and the tigers. His favorite animal is the giraffe. Sometimes he gets to feed the ducks. He loves to go to the zoo.

---

1. Who likes to go to the zoo?

(A) Jack

(B) Jill

(C) Jason

2. What is his favorite animal?

(A) the giraffe

(B) the tiger

(C) the monkey

3. What does he get to do sometimes?

(A) feed the pigs

(B) feed the horses

(C) feed the ducks

Shopping

**Carlos likes to go shopping with his
mom. Sometimes she lets him hold the list.
He helps her look for things they need like
bananas and green beans. It is fun to go
shopping with his mom.**

1. What does Carlos like to do?
Ⓐ   go to the zoo with his dad
Ⓑ   go shopping with his mom
Ⓒ   go to school

2. What does he get to hold
sometimes?
Ⓐ   the list
Ⓑ   the cart
Ⓒ   the bananas

3. What does he help her look for?
Ⓐ   things they need like
bananas and green beans
Ⓑ   toys
Ⓒ   cookies and candy

Name_____

Making Cookies

**Sally likes to help her mom make cookies.
She helps put the flour into the bowl. She
helps stir the batter. She likes licking the
beater. The best part is eating the cookies
when they are done.**

1. Who likes to make cookies?
Ⓐ Sam
Ⓑ Sally
Ⓒ Sarah

2. What does she stir?
Ⓐ the flour
Ⓑ the sugar
Ⓒ the batter

3. What is the best part?
Ⓐ pouring the flour
Ⓑ eating the cookies when
    they are done
Ⓒ stirring the batter

Raking Leaves

**Raking leaves can be fun. Jim puts a lot
of leaves in a very big pile. When it gets
really big, he jumps into the pile. Then
he has to rake it up again.**

1. What can be fun?

(A) raking leaves

(B) mowing the lawn

(C) pulling weeds

2. Where does Jim put the leaves?

(A) on the porch

(B) in a bag

(C) in a very big pile

3. What does he do when he has a big pile?

(A) jumps into it

(B) walks around it

(C) leaves it alone

Name_____

Robins

Robins live in a nest. The nest sits in a tree. The robin keeps its eggs safe in the nest.

---

1. Where does a robin live?
Ⓐ   in a car
Ⓑ   in a nest
Ⓒ   in a house

2. Where is the nest?
Ⓐ   in a tree
Ⓑ   in a house
Ⓒ   on a street

3. Where are the eggs?
Ⓐ   in the nest
Ⓑ   on the road
Ⓒ   in a house

Winter

**Winter is cold. Sometimes it snows.
You can wear a hat and gloves. You can
make a snowman. Winter can be fun.**

---

1. What happens sometimes in winter?

    Ⓐ   It snows.

    Ⓑ   It is hot.

    Ⓒ   It is humid.

2. What do you wear in winter?

    Ⓐ   shorts

    Ⓑ   hat and gloves

    Ⓒ   a swimsuit

3. What can you make in winter?

    Ⓐ   a sand castle

    Ⓑ   a snowman

    Ⓒ   a leaf pile

Name_____

Turtles

Some turtles are green. Turtles are very slow. Turtles have shells.

1. How do turtles move?
   (A) slow
   (B) fast

2. What do turtles have?
   (A) tents
   (B) houses
   (C) shells

3. What color are some turtles?
   (A) yellow
   (B) green
   (C) blue

Firefighters

Firefighters have hard jobs because they fight fires. They always have to be ready to go to a fire. They race to the fire in their fire truck.

1. What do firefighters do?
- Ⓐ teach math
- Ⓑ catch people doing something wrong
- Ⓒ fight fires

2. When do firefighters have to be ready to go to a fire?
- Ⓐ all the time
- Ⓑ when they feel like it
- Ⓒ only in the daytime

3. How do they get to the fire?
- Ⓐ in a car
- Ⓑ they run
- Ⓒ in the fire truck

Name_____

Dump Truck

Dump trucks are fun to watch. Sometimes they carry dirt to a job site. Other times they take dirt away from a job site. Then they dump the dirt out of their trays onto the ground.

---

1. What do dump trucks carry to a job site?
- Ⓐ grass
- Ⓑ food
- Ⓒ dirt

2. Where do they dump the dirt?
- Ⓐ up in the air
- Ⓑ under a building
- Ⓒ on the ground

3. From the story, what is a tray?
- Ⓐ a motor
- Ⓑ a back part of a dump truck

Mail Truck

A mail truck is full of letters for people.
The truck picks up the letters from the post
office. It brings them to the mailboxes.

---

1. What does a mail truck carry?

Ⓐ food

Ⓑ letters

Ⓒ ice cream

2. Where does the mail truck bring
the letters from?

Ⓐ the post office

Ⓑ the grocery store

Ⓒ the library

3. Where does the mail truck bring
the letters to?

Ⓐ the mailboxes

Ⓑ the park

Ⓒ the backyard

Name_____

Rain

Rain is wet and cold. It makes puddles on the ground. Sometimes you can see a rainbow after it rains.

---

1. What does rain feel like?

Ⓐ wet

Ⓑ dry

2. What does the rain make on the ground?

Ⓐ dirt

Ⓑ pictures

Ⓒ puddles

3. What do you see sometimes after it rains?

Ⓐ the night sky

Ⓑ storm clouds

Ⓒ a rainbow

Name_____

In Summer

It is hot in the summer. You can swim in the water to cool off. You can wear shorts, t-shirts, and sunglasses. You can play games outside like baseball and soccer. It is fun.

1. What does it feel like in the summer?

Ⓐ cold

Ⓑ hot

Ⓒ wet

2. What do you wear?

Ⓐ jackets

Ⓑ gloves and hats

Ⓒ shorts and sunglasses

3. What can you do to cool off?

Ⓐ swim in the water

Ⓑ run really fast

Ⓒ play games

Name_____

Bees

**Bees live in hives. They carry pollen
from flower to flower. They make honey.
Watch out! They can sting you.**

---

1. Where do bees live?

Ⓐ in a tree

Ⓑ in hives

Ⓒ in the grass

2. What do they carry from flower
to flower?

Ⓐ dirt

Ⓑ seeds

Ⓒ pollen

3. What do they make?

Ⓐ honey

Ⓑ candy

Ⓒ juice

Flowers

Flowers are parts of plants. They come in many shapes, sizes, and colors. Most flowers bloom in the spring. They are very pretty.

1. What are flowers part of?

Ⓐ   animals

Ⓑ   plants

Ⓒ   people

2. When do most flowers bloom?

Ⓐ   in the fall

Ⓑ   in the winter

Ⓒ   in the spring

3. What do they look like?

Ⓐ   pretty

Ⓑ   ugly

Name_____

The Farm

The farm is a fun place to visit. You can see horses, cows, and pigs on the farm. The farmer works very hard. He plants many crops so we can have food to eat.

1. What animals can you see on the farm?

   (A) tigers, lions, and bears

   (B) zebras, kangaroos, and giraffes

   (C) horses, cows, and pigs

2. Does the farmer work hard?

   (A) yes

   (B) no

3. Why does he plant crops?

   (A) so they can look pretty

   (B) so we have food to eat

   (C) It is fun.

28

Apples

Apples are round, hard, and juicy. They can be red, green, or yellow. They grow high up in the branches on trees. Fruits like apples are good foods for you to eat.

1. What color are apples?
Ⓐ orange, purple, and pink
Ⓑ white, blue, or black
Ⓒ red, green, or yellow

2. Where do they grow?
Ⓐ in the ground
Ⓑ down low
Ⓒ up high in the branches

3. Are they good for you to eat?
Ⓐ yes
Ⓑ no

Name_____

Trees

Trees are plants. Most of them are big
and tall. Trees have brown trunks and
many branches. They have green leaves.
Trees are homes for many animals like
birds and squirrels.

---

1. What are trees?
   - (A) plants
   - (B) animals
   - (C) people

2. What size are most trees?
   - (A) small
   - (B) short
   - (C) tall

3. What are trees homes for?
   - (A) cows
   - (B) birds and squirrels
   - (C) tigers

Ducks

**Ducks swim in the water. They have
webbed feet that help them swim. They
use their bills to get food out of the water.
Their babies are called ducklings.**

---

1. Where do ducks swim?

Ⓐ in the water

Ⓑ on the grass

Ⓒ in the dirt

2. What helps them get food out of
the water?

Ⓐ their feet

Ⓑ their wings

Ⓒ their bills

3. What are their babies called?

Ⓐ puppies

Ⓑ kittens

Ⓒ ducklings

Name_____

How to Play Hide and Seek

1. **Choose one person to be** *it*.
2. **That person counts to ten.**
3. **Everyone else hides.**
4. **The person who is** *it* **looks for everyone else.**

---

1. What number does the person who is *it* count to?
- Ⓐ forty
- Ⓑ ten

2. Why does the person count?
- Ⓐ to practice counting
- Ⓑ to give everyone time to hide
- Ⓒ to have fun

3. What does everyone else do?
- Ⓐ jumps
- Ⓑ runs
- Ⓒ hides

Taking Care of a Puppy

1. **Feed the puppy.**
2. **Give the puppy water.**
3. **Take the puppy on walks.**
4. **Play with the puppy.**

1. What are you supposed to give a puppy to drink?

Ⓐ   grape juice

Ⓑ   lemonade

Ⓒ   water

2. Where do you take the puppy?

Ⓐ   inside a store

Ⓑ   on walks

Ⓒ   to the library

3. What should you do with the puppy?

Ⓐ   play

Ⓑ   be rough

Ⓒ   leave it by itself

Name_____

What Flowers Need to Grow

1. **Flowers need sunshine to grow.**
2. **Flowers need water to grow.**
3. **Flowers need dirt to grow.**
4. **Some flowers take a lot of work to grow.**

---

1. What do flowers need to grow?

Ⓐ   dark

Ⓑ   sunshine

Ⓒ   clouds

2. What else do flowers need to grow?

Ⓐ   water

Ⓑ   worms

Ⓒ   bugs

3. Do some flowers take a lot of work to grow?

Ⓐ   yes

Ⓑ   no

Pool Rules

1. **No running by the pool.**
2. **No splashing in the pool.**
3. **Always swim with a grown–up.**

---

1. What is the first rule?

Ⓐ No running by the pool.

Ⓑ No playing in the pool.

Ⓒ No having fun in the pool.

2. What can you not do in the pool?

Ⓐ swim

Ⓑ splash

Ⓒ dive

3. Who do you always need to swim with?

Ⓐ a friend

Ⓑ a dog

Ⓒ a grown–up

Name_____

Setting the Table

1. **Put cups on the table.**

2. **Put plates and napkins on the table.**

3. **Put forks, spoons, and knives on the table.**

---

1. Where do you put the cups?

Ⓐ   on the table

Ⓑ   on the floor

Ⓒ   on the counter

2. Do the napkins go on the table before or after the forks, spoons, and knives?

Ⓐ   before

Ⓑ   after

3. Why do you set the table?

Ⓐ   to get ready for bed

Ⓑ   to get ready for school

Ⓒ   to get ready to eat

School Rules

1. **Raise your hand before you talk.**
2. **No talking when the teacher is talking.**
3. **No running inside the school.**
4. **Be kind to your friends.**

1. What do you do before you talk?

Ⓐ   Stand by your chair.

Ⓑ   Ask a friend.

Ⓒ   Raise your hand.

2. When can you not talk?

Ⓐ   at recess

Ⓑ   when the teacher is talking

Ⓒ   at lunch

3. What can you not do inside the school?

Ⓐ   run

Ⓑ   walk

Ⓒ   talk

Name_____

Packing My Backpack

1. **I put a folder in my backpack.**
2. **I put a lunch box in my backpack.**
3. **I put a book in my backpack.**
4. **Then I zip up my backpack.**

1. What do you put in your backpack?
- Ⓐ toys
- Ⓑ folder
- Ⓒ cookies

2. What else do you put in your backpack?
- Ⓐ lunch box
- Ⓑ candy
- Ⓒ a camera

3. What do you do last?
- Ⓐ Put something else in it.
- Ⓑ Leave it open.
- Ⓒ Zip it up.

Bedtime

1. **Put on your pajamas.**
2. **Brush your teeth.**
3. **Read a story.**
4. **Say good night.**

1. What do you do first at bedtime?

Ⓐ   Read a story.

Ⓑ   Say good night.

Ⓒ   Put on your pajamas.

2. What do you brush at bedtime?

Ⓐ   the dog's hair

Ⓑ   your teeth

Ⓒ   you mom's hair

3. What do you do last at bedtime?

Ⓐ   Say goodnight.

Ⓑ   Brush your teeth.

Ⓒ   Put on your pajamas.

Name_____

How to Have a Picnic

1. **Fix some good food to eat.**
2. **Put all of the food in a basket.**
3. **Bring the basket to a warm, sunny place.**
4. **Share the food with family or friends.**

1. What do you fix for a picnic?

Ⓐ toys

Ⓑ games

Ⓒ good food

2. Where do you put all of the food?

Ⓐ in a basket

Ⓑ in the house

Ⓒ on the table

3. Where do you take it to?

Ⓐ a friend's house

Ⓑ a warm, sunny place

Ⓒ the library

Doing Well in School

1. **Listen to your teacher.**
2. **Come to school every day.**
3. **Do your best work.**

---

1. Who do you need to listen to at school?

Ⓐ your friend

Ⓑ your teacher

Ⓒ your letter carrier

2. How often do you need to come to school?

Ⓐ every day

Ⓑ once a week

Ⓒ when you feel like it

3. What kind of work do you need to do?

Ⓐ sloppy

Ⓑ fast

Ⓒ your best

Name_____

Baking a Birthday Cake

1. Mix the batter in a bowl.
2. Pour the batter in a pan.
3. Bake the cake in the oven.
4. Spread frosting on the cake.
5. Share the cake with your family and friends.

1. What do you mix the batter in?
- Ⓐ a cup
- Ⓑ a bowl
- Ⓒ a pan

2. What do you bake the cake in?
- Ⓐ the oven
- Ⓑ the freezer
- Ⓒ the microwave

3. What do you spread on top of the cake?
- Ⓐ jelly
- Ⓑ peanut butter
- Ⓒ frosting

Going Camping

1. **Set up a tent.**
2. **Take long hikes to see birds, animals, and trees.**
3. **Build a fire in the fire pit.**
4. **Roast hot dogs and marshmallows over the fire.**

1. What do you need to set up when you camp?

Ⓐ   a playhouse

Ⓑ   a tent

Ⓒ   a table

2. What do you take long hikes to see?

Ⓐ   people

Ⓑ   houses

Ⓒ   birds, animals, and trees

3. Where do you build a fire?

Ⓐ   in the fire pit

Ⓑ   by the tent

Ⓒ   by a tree

Name_____

Tag

1. **Choose a child to be** *it*.
2. **Start running away fast.**
3. **The child who is** *it* **runs after everyone.**
4. **The one he tags is** *it*.

---

1. What is the first step to play tag?
  Ⓐ Start running away fast.
  Ⓑ The one he tags is *it*.
  Ⓒ Choose a child to be *it*.

2. When someone is *it*, what do you do?
  Ⓐ Start running away fast.
  Ⓑ Start walking slowly.
  Ⓒ Start sneaking away quietly.

3. Who is *it* next?
  Ⓐ the one who falls
  Ⓑ the one who is slowest
  Ⓒ the one he tags

44

Making a Card

1. **Fold a piece of paper.**
2. **Draw a picture on the front of the card.**
3. **Write a note on the inside.**
4. **Give it to someone special.**

1. What do you use to make a card?

Ⓐ   a piece of paper

Ⓑ   a book

Ⓒ   a toy

2. What do you do with the front of the card?

Ⓐ   Write your name.

Ⓑ   Put your fingerprint.

Ⓒ   Draw a picture.

3. Who do you give the card to?

Ⓐ   someone you do not know

Ⓑ   someone special

Ⓒ   someone who is mean to you

Name_____

Answer Sheet

Practice	Practice

Title

1. Ⓐ Ⓑ Ⓒ

2. Ⓐ Ⓑ Ⓒ

3. Ⓐ Ⓑ Ⓒ

Title

1. Ⓐ Ⓑ Ⓒ

2. Ⓐ Ⓑ Ⓒ

3. Ⓐ Ⓑ Ⓒ

Practice	Practice

Title

1. Ⓐ Ⓑ Ⓒ

2. Ⓐ Ⓑ Ⓒ

3. Ⓐ Ⓑ Ⓒ

Title

1. Ⓐ Ⓑ Ⓒ

2. Ⓐ Ⓑ Ⓒ

3. Ⓐ Ⓑ Ⓒ

Answer Key

The Birthday Party, page 4
1. a
2. b
3. a

Camping, page 5
1. a
2. b
3. b

The New Bike, page 6
1. b
2. c
3. b

The Cat in the Tree, page 7
1. a
2. a
3. b

The Balloon, page 8
1. b
2. c
3. a

Puppies for Sale, page 9
1. a
2. a
3. b

Clouds, page 10
1. b
2. b
3. c

Lost and Found, page 11
1. c
2. a
3. c

David's First Baseball Game, page 12
1. c
2. b
3. a

Camping in the Backyard, page 13
1. b
2. c
3. a

A Trip to the Zoo, page 14
1. c
2. a
3. c

Shopping, page 15
1. b
2. a
3. a

Making Cookies, page 16
1. b
2. c
3. b

Raking Leaves, page 17
1. a
2. c
3. a

Robbins, page 18
1. b
2. a
3. a

Winter, page 19
1. a
2. b
3. b

Turtles, page 20
1. a
2. c
3. b

Firefighters, page 21
1. c
2. a
3. c

Dump Truck, page 22
1. c
2. c
3. b

Mail Truck, page 23
1. b
2. a
3. a

Rain, page 24
1. a
2. c
3. c

Answer Key (cont.)

In Summer, page 25
1. b
2. c
3. a

Bees, page 26
1. b
2. c
3. a

Flowers, page 27
1. b
2. c
3. a

The Farm, page 28
1. c
2. a
3. b

Apples, page 29
1. c
2. c
3. a

Trees, page 30
1. a
2. c
3. b

Ducks, page 31
1. a
2. c
3. c

How to Play Hide and Seek, page 32
1. b
2. b
3. c

Taking Care of a Puppy, page 33
1. c
2. b
3. a

What Flowers Need to Grow, page 34
1. b
2. a
3. a

Pool Rules, page 35
1. a
2. b
3. c

Setting the Table, page 36
1. a
2. a
3. c

School Rules, page 37
1. c
2. b
3. a

Packing My Backpack, page 38
1. b
2. a
3. c

Bedtime, page 39
1. c
2. b
3. a

How to Have a Picnic, page 40
1. c
2. a
3. b

Doing Well in School, page 41
1. b
2. a
3. c

Baking a Birthday Cake, page 42
1. b
2. a
3. c

Going Camping, page 43
1. b
2. c
3. a

Tag, page 44
1. c
2. a
3. c

Making a Card, page 45
1. a
2. c
3. b